CHARLIE BUBBLES
TO FENWAY!

Written by Paul Carafotes

Story by Charles Carafotes

Illustrated by Jeff Vernon

Special thanks to The Boston Red Sox and Major League Baseball

Very special thanks to Mark Jenest

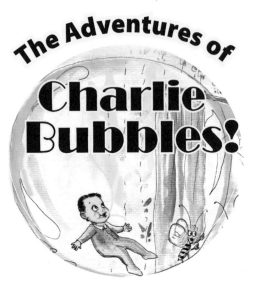

www.charliebubblesbook.com
Like us at Facebook.com/TheAdventuresOfCharlieBubbles
Follow us at Twitter @charliebubbles5
and @carafotes12

SUMMARY: The adventures continue in "Charlie Bubbles to Fenway!" Charlie overcomes adversity by believing in himself, showing courage and dreaming big dreams.

K-4 Fun for the whole family.

Author's Note

When you say yes, anything is possible. When you say no, nothing happens.

When we were preparing "Charlie Bubbles 2 SMARTSVILLE!" to go to print, my son
Charlie came to me and sweetly asked, "Dad, will there be a third Charlie Bubbles
book?" I was stumped because I never saw past the first book,
"The Adventures of Charlie Bubbles!" My aim was to give my son a gift,
one that he might pass along to his children one day. So when he asked me that
question I looked him in the eye and said, "Yes, there will be a third book
and you're going to help write it." I could see that this perplexed him. "Me?" he
asked. Then I said, "What should it be about?" Without hesitation he replied,
"Charlie Bubbles to Fenway!" He loves the Red Sox and baseball, just as I do.
This book is about dreaming big dreams and believing in yourself.
We hope you enjoy it.

Drawing by Charlie

It was a crisp, cool spring day. Charlie was on a frozen pond, learning how to skate and wondering how in the world a baseball player like himself could ever skate. His teacher was his friend, Tai the Butterfly.

Charlie would rather watch her than do any actual skating.

"On your skates Bubble Boy," said Tai.

"Can you do that triple axle thing and spread your butterfly wings at the end?" Charlie asked.

"Not until you skate to me. Come on," urged Tai.

<big>H</big>e got up, took a step, and fell.

"You can do it, Charlie!"

He got right back up and tried again. This time he took two steps and fell. Three crows watched Charlie, snickering from the edge of the pond. Their leader was mean and nasty.

"Look at that silly boy," said the leader. "He can't skate. He's useless. Haha," the crows laughed.

Charlie was embarrassed.

"Hey kid, maybe you should try something else. Learn to fall better." The crows cackled with delight.

"Don't listen to them, Charlie. I'm positive they can't skate," said Tai.

"Watch out butterfly, or we'll take you to our nest and feed you to our brothers and sisters," said the leader.

"Bullies is what you are! Go, fly away and leave us alone," cried Tai the Butterfly. "You can do it, Charlie."

"I'll bet he hasn't got the courage to do it," said the nasty leader.

Charlie was full of fear and confusion now.

Then he remembered what his dad had said to him, that sometimes when you felt fear you had to try and do it anyway. That's what courage was. He took a deep breath.

Tai spread her amazing wings and smiled at Charlie.

"You have to believe in yourself. Do you believe in you?" Tai asked.

The Bubble Boy wasn't sure. He got up, but again tumbled to the ice. Now the crows fell about with laughter.

Then from somewhere deep inside, courage and belief bubbled up in Charlie. This time he focused. His feet were steady and balanced. He blew three bubbles, and suddenly he was skating. Bubbles are magic.

Tai clapped her wings, whirled around, and fluttered two feet off the ice.

Teddy Hiccup and Paulie Pumpkin arrived.
"We've got skates here for you three bird brains to see
how well *you* can do," Teddy hiccuped.
Now it was the crows turn to quiver with fear.

"We can't skate," said the crows. "We fly."
"Then may we suggest that you either learn to play nice and be friendly,
or fly away," piped Paulie.
So they flew away.

"Did you see? Did you see me skate?" Charlie bubbled with pride.
"You're going to be an excellent skater. And you were very brave
too!" fluttered Tai.
"I was afraid, but I knew I had to try."

Teddy hiccups, "It's April, and you know what that means."
"Baseball!" shouted Charlie, as he blew his magic bubble for lift off.
He had to get home. He knew today was an extra special day.

Charlie laid down and closed his eyes. He began to daydream...

Charlie dreamed about his favorite team, the Red Sox. He was born in 2007. The Red Sox won the world series that year and had just won it again. He closed his eyes and saw the most beautiful ballpark in all the world: Fenway!

He could smell the freshly cut grass, the field smooth and perfect.

And the Green Monster. He dreamed of hitting balls over it onto Landsdown street. He, Pedroia, and Big Papi. Teammates, buddies, and pals.

It was opening day. Charlie was playing shortstop.

He and Pedroia were playing catch. Johnny Gomes high fived him on his way out to left field.

Big Papi stood on the steps of the dugout and pointed at Charlie with that big, friendly smile. Charlie was having an awesome dream...

...and it all seemed so real!

The umpire called, "Play ball!" The fans rose to their feet. Charlie's mom and dad were cheering. Jacoby Ellsbury stepped in to the batter's box.
Now, this was really weird. Ellsbury didn't look right in Yankee pinstripes, thought Charlie.

Suddenly there was a ball hit to his left. He went after it, but it was deeper than he thought. The Green Monster was getting closer and closer. If he didn't do something soon it could be a double bubble, bash and crash into the wall.

Charlie blew a magic bubble. He floated up, up, up towards the ball. He reached out. He stretched as far as he could, and caught the ball. A fantastic grab. The crowd cheered wildly.

He was so excited that he didn't realize he had burst his bubble.
"Uh-oh!" said Charlie.

He began to fall. Falling faster and faster. He didn't know what to do.
He tried to blow another bubble but couldn't. He was just about to hit the
ground when...

...the three crows swooped down and gently caught him.

"Great catch Charlie," chirped the leader.
"Where'd you guys come from?" asked a very surprised and thankful Charlie.

"We went to the pond and tried to skate. It was really, really hard. We thought about how much courage you showed and how badly we behaved, so we came back to say we're sorry."

"Awwww, you dudes are way cool. Thanks for saving me."

The crowd began to chant, "Charlie Bubbles! Charlie Bubbles! Charlie…"

A voice called softly, "Charlie? Charlie? Wake up, son."

Charlie opened his eyes. His dad was smiling at him. "Did you forget that it's opening day at Fenway?"
"How could I ever forget that, dad?"
"Then what are you doing being a sleepy head? Let's go!"

"Dad, can I ask you a question?"

"Ask me anything, son."

Charlie thought hard. "Naw, forget it dad. It's really stupid."

"Charlie, there are no stupid questions."

"Ok, here goes. Will there be crows at Fenway?"

His father laughed. "No crows. Yankees! Get your glove. The Red Sox await their future second baseman."

"I changed my mind. I believe I want to play shortstop," Charlie announced.

His dad looked into his little boy's eyes.

"Charlie, if you believe you can do it, then you can. You can do anything you put your mind to. Make it happen in your dreams and it'll happen in your life."

This time Charlie laughed. "I already know that, dad."

"Attaboy," his father said with a wink. "Let's go. I can hardly wait for a hot dog."

"It's going to be bubblishous," said Charlie.

So off they went, father and son, happily to Fenway.

Get Your Copies of the First Two
Bubble Experiences!
To order visit

amazon.com or charliebubblesbook.com

Follow us on Twitter @charliebubbles5 Facebook/TheAdventuresOfCharlieBubbles

"One of the more imaginative and visually stunning children's books to come out this year is THE ADVENTURES OF CHARLIE BUBBLES! This sensitive and entertaining story is not only full of rich meaning for children to absorb in building solid personalities and philosophies but also is a beautiful little fable about friendship."
-- Grady Harp, Hall of Fame Reviewer,
    Amazon and Good Reads

"Charlie Bubbles is soon to be a classic.
I've read it several times and
keep re-reading it.
That's a sign that something
is good and will last."
-- James Gandolfini, Father and actor

PAUL CARAFOTES, a single dad, has been an award winning actor, writer and director for more than 30 years appearing in numerous movies, television shows and commercials. He has won various entertainment awards, such as best writer for his play "Beyond The Ring", as well as his film "Club Soda" which has won multiple awards throughout the country. "Charlie Bubbles to Fenway!" is Paul's third children's book in the Charlie Bubbles series. The critically acclaimed first book, "The Adventures of Charlie Bubbles!" and "Charlie Bubbles 2 Smartsville!" were inspired by Paul's son Charlie. You can learn more by liking Paul on his Facebook page and following him on Twitter @carafotes12.

The author pictured with his inspiration, Charlie.

Drawing by Charlie.

JEFF VERNON has worked as a graphic designer and illustrator for over 35 years. He has worked for numerous ad agencies, designing packaging for ATARI, and art studios creating innovative artwork including promotional key art for movies and television as well as two musical children's books. Jeff has illustrated six children's books for Veronica Lane Books and best-selling author Etan Boritzer as part of the *"What Is?"* series. This is Jeff's third collaboration with friend Paul, who he met in Hollywood in 1981. See more of Jeff's work at jeffvernon.com.